Success Principles That Really Work
Learn in 30 Minutes How to Succeed in the Workplace
By Bruce L Kirby

Copyright 2016 Bruce L. Kirby

All rights reserved

Printed in the United States of America

Contents

Introduction 4

Preface 6

Personal Values I Was Raised By 12

Measurement of Success 19

Management vs. Leadership 22

My Basic Principles for Success in the Workplace. 24

    Three A's (Ability, Availability and Affability) 24

    Three B's (Boldness, Beneficial and Belief) 45

    Three C's (Communication, Coordination and Cooperation) 48

Conclusion 56

Outline Summary (tear out section) 57

Introduction

This booklet is being written in a format that is easy to read and remember. My intent is to lay out my basic principles for success in the workplace in this edition based on my life experiences in a broad easy-to-absorb format. I've read so many publications about principles that lose the main concepts in a conglomeration of "use up space" rhetoric, so I decided to write a publication in an "easy-to-recall" outline format. These principles can be beneficial not only to the white collar executive level manager but also the blue collar employee who works "where the rubber meets the road". I encourage the reader to think about each principle as it relates to his or her present approach to the workplace and to contemplate how it might impact or change his or her approach in the future. Contingent upon appropriate demand, I plan to follow on with subsequent publications that will elaborate on each principle and provide more of a detailed guide, with real life examples, for those who may be starting their careers and who have not yet established their "roadmap" to career success. I am assuming, though, that most readers will have already established a foundation for their approach to the workplace and may just need a little more insight or wisdom as to how they may "fine tune" that approach.

Preface

Now, one might ask at this point why I think I am qualified to write this publication? The following autobiographical summary will hopefully convince you of my qualifications and that I certainly have been "around the block a few times" in terms of learning from my own experiences as well as those experiences from others with whom I have observed or read about during my 40 plus year career. This booklet is a compilation of those principles that I have tested throughout my working career and have labeled as principles that really work. If you are still skeptical at the end of this preface that I have not had success in the workplace and that I am not qualified to write this, then I suggest you simply not read any further.

I was raised in a small town along the short coast of New Hampshire. My parents believed in strong family values where all life's activities, business and pleasure, benefited the family and were only executed with the family's best interests in mind. My Dad was a very successful businessman who founded and built a company, without a formal education, through hard work, perseverance and devotion to his values, both professional and family. My Dad was one of the heroes in my life with whom I based the starting foundation of my own success in the workplace.

- My School Years:
    - Graduated from High School with honors as a member of the National Honor Society.
    - Although not an athletic super-star, I lettered in the varsity team sports of football, basketball and track and field and became relatively proficient in the individual sport of tennis.
    - Very active in extracurricular activities such as music and art. I was a part time professional trumpet player at the age of 17,

which certainly helped supplement the cost of my forthcoming college education by performing in various jazz and dance band ensembles.
- Graduated from a state university with a BS degree in Business Administration.
- Graduated from a US Army affiliated post graduate program and earned a MS degree in Healthcare Administration while on active duty with the US Army Medical Department.

- My Military Career – US Army:
    - Participated in two wars, one during my junior years as a Combat Medical Platoon Leader in the Republic of Vietnam (see my book entitled "Faces of the Dead and the Dying – Memories of a Vietnam Combat Medic" available through Amazon) and one during my senior years as the medical

staffing and recruiting advisor to the Army Surgeon General during the declared war in the Persian Gulf, Desert Storm.
- Mid-career, I graduated from the US Army Command and General Staff College.
- I served in various senior staff officer positions both at the US Army Medical Command in San Antonio, Texas, and at The Army Surgeon General's Office in Washington, DC.
- I rounded out my 20 year military career assigned to the Surgeon General's Office but attached to the US Army Forces Command in Atlanta, Georgia where I began my transition into my civilian career.

- My Civilian Career:
  - With a strong Army background in healthcare staffing and human resources

management, I started my civilian career as a physician recruiter with one of the oldest and largest medical staffing firms in the civilian sector and ended up as the chief executive for another one of the largest medical staffing companies in the country.

- I retired from "Corporate America" 10 years later only to find myself embarking on a third career venture in healthcare development and administration.

- Most Recent Positions:
    - Chief Executive Officer, facility developer and equity partner in a 100 plus physician multispecialty clinic.
    - Chief Executive Officer and majority equity partner in a medical staffing services company

- - Healthcare Operations advisor to an international development company embarking on its first South American hospital development project.
  - Board member and advisor to a variety of other organizations, both business and civic.
- My Family:
  - Married over 40 years to a very career supportive spouse
  - 2 children and one grandchild

With a successful personal life spanning over 60 years and a successful working life spanning over 40 years, I think I have the experience, the credentials and the qualifications to elaborate on the essential elements necessary, in my opinion, to experience success in the workplace.

Personal Values I Was Raised By

As mentioned previously, my parents possessed strong family values, unfortunately an American attribute dissipating in today's society (but that is a topic for another time). Here are the values that I was raised by:

- Honesty – I was taught that a lie would always catch up to you usually with negative impact. Although sometimes the truth may hurt, in the long run you will always come out ahead if the truth is revealed at the outset. Throughout my childhood I remember very vividly that when I was caught in a lie by trying to hide the truth, the consequences would be much worse than if I had told the truth at the outset. It did not take me very long to learn this valuable lesson.
- Integrity – Throughout my life I've noticed a gradual decrease in this trait within America, especially in business. One thing I can say about the military (at least when I was on active duty – not too sure about

today's military), integrity was a feature that was prevalent among the ranks, both non-commissioned and commissioned officers ranks. I cannot say the same about the civilian sector. It became obvious to me early on that greed was the main driver for behavior in the civilian world. I've encountered many throughout my civilian career who would, without hesitation, compromise their integrity if it meant furthering their personal gain, whether it was for money or for power. One of the best examples of the prevalence of integrity in America goes back to my Dad who built a very successful business during the years between post World War II and the late 1980's. Because of my Dad's stellar reputation as an honest businessman and the extraordinary value of his word, every contract he entered into was sealed with a simple handshake – never a formal written contract or agreement. As we all know, with the epidemic of today's aspiring attorneys setting out to make their fortunes by complicating our business world with mountains of written documents filled with their own language that only they can understand, the days of contractual handshakes and the value of one's word are approaching extinction.

- Loyalty – No matter what the temptation may be to be unfaithful to a superior, a colleague, a subordinate, a mentor or a family member, it should be resisted at all cost, assuming, of course, that your faithfulness does not sanction an act that is illegal, unprofessional or unethical. Loyalty should be paramount in all relationships, even if the immediate consequences are sometimes not the most desirable. In the long term, you will be glad that you chose to be loyal because you will find that the ultimate benefit to you will outweigh any benefit that could have been attained by being disloyal.

- Self-discipline – If you are the kind of person who needs to be told by someone how and when to act upon a situation or a potential situation, whether it be in your job or in your family, then you need to develop the trait of self-discipline. In most cases, most know what, when and how to do something in a particular situation but, for whatever reason, decide to either hesitate, wait to be told or simply not act at all. It is better to be pro-active to an anticipated situation and to act before the consequences become undesirable than to be reactive to a situation when it may very well be too late to experience a desirable outcome. Lack of self-discipline can cause considerable issues in one's workplace and certainly delay any forward movement towards success.
- Work Ethic – In my opinion, honest hard work is another dissipating trait within American societies. It seems to me that the majority of today's working

Americans want huge pay checks but do not want to work for those huge checks. My Dad taught me that hard work never hurt anyone, whether it is in blue collar or white collar work. I'm not saying that today's generation is lazy but there seems to be a definite trend of people who want to work less for more compensation. Do not confuse this with the concept of working smart. Working efficiently by leveraging one's resources is always better than working inefficiently.

- Respect - There is so much disrespect in today's societies it almost makes me wonder if I am living in the right country. I see it every day from young children disrespecting their parents, to young students disrespecting their teachers, to young adults disrespecting their elders and to employees disrespecting their bosses. True, respect has to be earned and not assumed, but, again, it seems to be a declining trait.

- Trust – This goes hand in hand with honesty, integrity and respect. Unless you can trust someone in a relationship, there is no relationship. Without honesty, integrity and respect there can be no trust.
- Perseverance – The old cliché of "if you do not succeed try try again", has merit. So many folks today give up so easily on a particular goal or objective and then wonder why they cannot achieve success. My favorite saying is "it is better to try and fail than fail to try". Believe me, for every failure you will experience two or more successes, assuming you learn from every failure and be persistent in achieving your goals.
- Spiritual Faith – I don't care what your religion is but you must believe in a Devine being or energy that controls the universe and the destinies of your life. If

nothing else, this belief can provide the edge you need to believe and be confident in yourself so you may accomplish your success in not only the workplace, but also life.

Measurement of Success

The first answer by most, especially in the business world, to the question: "How do you measure success?" would be "monetary wealth". Well, I beg to differ. Although an individual with a lot of money may be perceived as successful, but until you know how and when that money was acquired, you really do not know if that individual is truly successful. The money could have been inherited or won by playing the lottery. The individual is certainly lucky by being in the right place at the right time, but can that really be termed as success? I believe that success should be measured simply by accomplishment. Some professions do not generate financial independence or wealth. Teaching is a good example. To say a teacher without wealth is not successful knowing that he or she has influenced the development of hundreds of students' minds, is absolutely ludicrous. Another good example is a career soldier, airman, sailor or coastguardsman. Our military certainly accomplish a great deal in their jobs but, obviously, do not gain wealth while a member of the armed forces. First responders (firemen, policemen and medics) by saving life, limb and property do not become wealthy but certainly accomplish a great deal during their careers. An onsite construction foreman, as another example, supervising the building of a 30 floor city sky scraper will not become wealthy doing his or her job but can certainly look at the successful completion of the building as his or her accomplishment.

As I write this publication and come to the end of my career, I am comfortable financially, but not wealthy. I obviously did not gain a great deal of wealth during my military career but I did achieve a tremendous sense of accomplishment and gained a great deal of experience and confidence.

Management vs. Leadership

Management and Leadership.

- **Management** in all business and organizational activities is the act of getting people together to accomplish desired goals and objectives using available resources efficiently and effectively. Since organizations can be viewed as systems, management can also be defined as human action, including design, to facilitate the production of useful outcomes from a system. This view opens the opportunity to 'manage' oneself, a pre-requisite to attempting to manage others.

- **Leadership** is a process of social influence in which one person can enlist the aid and support of others in the accomplishment of a common task. Effective leadership is the ability to successfully integrate and maximize available resources within the internal and external environment for the attainment of organizational or societal goals. I have termed effective leadership as "persuasive influence". The act of persuading someone to want to work for you or with you to accomplish your goals is effective leadership.

My Basic Principles for Success in the Workplace.

Three A's (Ability, Availability and Affability)

- **Ability** (probably my most important principle for success)
    - **Attitude + Motivation + Knowledge = Ability to Succeed**
        - **Attitude** - You must always have a positive attitude towards everything you do, particularly in the workplace. I believe that performing by intimidation no longer works in today's societies. Persuasive influence (or leadership) is a much more effective tool and can maximize the potential of people resources. Those around you, whether superior or subordinate, can be influenced and encouraged by your positive attitude,

even when the issues surrounding a particular adverse situation may seem hopeless and unsolvable.

- **Motivation** – Remaining consistently motivated to do what is necessary to achieve your goals is paramount. To come up with ideas or plans is much easier than actually turning those ideas into actions or executing those plans. The greatest idea in the world or the greatest plan in the world is worthless if one does not have the motivation to execute it.
- **Knowledge** - Knowledge is key. Without complete knowledge of a particular task you are trying to accomplish, unless you are lucky, you will not succeed. Knowledge is power. If you feel you do not have enough knowledge or

information to achieve a certain goal then seek it from those who do. There is nothing wrong with capitalizing on the expertise of others. Proceeding or making a decision without sufficient knowledge could lead to failure instead of success.

- **Capitalize on the talents of others**
  - It is impossible to be all knowing. Don't let pride, ego or stubbornness stand in the way of your success. So many potentially successful people are seriously handicapped by their inability to be humble and to confer with those who they know are better versed on a particular topic. By doing so you not only gain the respect and admiration of others, but you also achieve your successes with much

less difficulty and much greater satisfaction.

- **Earn respect and confidence of others**.
  - Make people <u>want</u> to work for or with you and not <u>have</u> to work for or with you. Persuade others to assist you. Do not insist, demand or intimidate as it only causes stress, resentment and resistance. An intimidation environment is non-conducive to maximum productivity.
- **Maintain high motivation and a positive attitude**.
  - Strive to sustain high morale, esprit de corps, pride and organizational loyalty. High morale promulgates production. Look forward to going to work every day. To do so, the following conditions must be prevalent. If one or more of these

conditions are lacking, sit down with the appropriate person to discuss your concerns.

- Economic security – You should be confident that you will be rewarded fairly for your time and effort.
- Emotional Security – You should have trust and feel that your accomplishments are contributive to the overall goals of the organization.
- Recognition – You should be recognized appropriately when warranted. A simple "thank you" or "good job" from the right person can go a long way.

- Self-respect – You should be treated as an individual, as a human being and not just a number. You should always be confident and feel good about what you do.
- Self-expression – You should feel free to communicate ideas, suggestions, fears and opinions without fear of retribution.

o **Know what all employees do in an organization.**
- Know all employees roles (superiors, peers and subordinates) and how they fit into the big picture of the organization.

o **Sustain Honesty and Integrity.**
- Honesty in the workplace

- Be honest with yourself as well as others.
- Being honest means choosing not to lie, steal, cheat or deceive in any way.
- Be sincere, truthful, trustworthy, fair, genuine and loyal with integrity.
- When being honest, you build strength of character that will allow you to be of greater service.
- Dishonesty harms you and harms others.
- Always accept responsibility for your own actions; don't blame others.

- Being honest will enhance your future opportunities and your ability to succeed.
- Be honest in your job by giving a full amount of work for your pay.
- Do not rationalize that being dishonest is acceptable, even though others may think it does not matter.

- Integrity in the workplace.
    - Integrity goes hand in hand with honesty.
    - Think and do what is right at all times, no matter what the consequences.
    - When you have integrity, you are willing to live by your standards,

beliefs and values even when no one is watching.
- Choose to live so your thoughts and behavior are always in harmony within the guidelines of absolute integrity.

o **Loyalty and Dedication**
- Loyalty - Fostering workplace loyalty is important.
    - Practice open and honest communication. Having the trust of your workplace culture will ensure people will believe what you have to say, and the ideas you wish to convey are ones you truly believe in.
    - Become connected with the other people in your workplace. Talk

with them. Ask for input on your ideas about various work tasks and activities. However, be cautious that your ideas are not stolen by someone who lacks integrity and are claimed as his or her own ideas.

- Create a collaborative culture. Today's workers want to feel that their opinions matter, that they can offer their unique perspectives and use their honed talents to align with others.
- Show appreciation for new ideas.
- Dedication in the workplace
    - Be punctual – Arriving late gives the impression that you do not

respect your colleagues, your subordinates or your superiors.

- Attendance – Do not abuse your sick days by taking them off when you are not sick. If you are sick or becoming sick, it is better to go in to work and then asked to be released (assuming the illness is not too serious or contagious)
- Time management – Good time management illustrates efficiency and that you are dedicated to your job
- Pride in your work – Do your job to the best of your ability and your performance will exude dedication.
- Show initiative – Be a self-starter. Be sure it is known that you do not

need prodding when it comes to doing your job.

- Stay busy – If you have times when there is little to do, ask around to see if there is something you can do to help someone else. You are being paid for your time so wasting that time shows lack of dedication.

- Company time vs. personal time – When you are at work you should be doing work. You should not be doing personal things while at work unless you are on an authorized break. No personal phone calls, texting, surfing the web, checking social media, involvement in personal chit chat with others, etc. This portrays you as being less dedicated to your work.

- Going above and beyond. Being willing to go above and beyond the call of duty will win you recognition and show that you appreciate the opportunity of having a job. This does not mean that you are living to work. But it does show that you are willing to give a little extra time to get things done.
- Flexibility – Being flexible is by far the most recognizable attribute you can possess. Go with the flow and handle fast changes. It will be

known that you can be depended upon in the pinch.

- Being a dedicated worker is really about showing a strong work ethic. You can be dedicated without throwing your life away to your job. Go to work. Do your job well. Avoid common workplace pitfalls like spreading gossip. Be willing to go the extra mile and go with the flow. At the end of the day, you will feel better about yourself and your job.

o **Fairness to all**.
- Do not show favoritism.
- Everyone should receive an equal opportunity to be heard and recognized.

- All personnel actions at work should be handled fairly and equitably. Do all that you can to reaffirm this with your colleagues, subordinates and superiors.
- Be transparent and committal when doing your job.

o **Lead by example**
  - Following are some famous quotes that address this concept:
    - "Nothing so conclusively proves a man's ability to lead others, as what he does from day to day to lead himself."
    - "If given the responsibility, take charge! Do what is right!"
    - "Setting an example is not the main means of influencing others, it is the only means."

- "Nothing speaks like results. If you want to build the kind of credibility that connects with people, then deliver results before you deliver the message. Get out and do what you advise others to do. Communicate from experience."
  - **Capitalize on lessons learned** – Do not make the same mistake twice. Everyone makes mistakes and that is acceptable under most circumstances, as long as you learn by those mistakes and do not keep repeating the same mistakes. Also, always admit your mistakes and apologize to those affected by it, if appropriate.
  - **KISS – Keep It Super Simple.** This concept has been around for a long time. So many people make a task or activity more complex than it needs to be. Always seek the simplest and most

efficient method of doing something, as long as that method results in the outcomes you desire. This not only saves you time but also eliminates the difficulty, the frustration and the stress that is associated with a complex task.

- **Micro-management should be avoided.** Enough trust and confidence should be prevalent among superiors, peers and subordinates so micro-management becomes unnecessary. Responsibility cannot be delegated to someone, but authority can be, providing the necessary tools are available to that someone to be able to complete a task and do his or her job. This will not only earn respect but also belief that one can be trusted enough to not be micro-managed. Everyone should have the appropriate autonomy to do their jobs. Treat everyone who is delegated the authority to complete a task or project the same way you would want to be treated if that same task or project was delegated to you. Following are suggestions for you to improve the delegation process:

- A problem should be delegated without the solution. The first sign of micro-management is when a project or task is delegated along with the specifics of the solution. This type of delegation does not enhance the skills of others and makes them feel limited in their approach to solving the problem or performing the assigned task.
- Experiences should be shared, not instructed. Experiences that have similar circumstances to the task that is being delegated should be shared. How the similar task was accomplished should be

shared but inference that there may be a better or more efficient way to complete the task should also be shared.

- If you are a manager delegating a task or a project, listen to progress, don't review it. When it comes time for progress to be reported, let folks report on the progress the way it works best for them. Provide feedback, don't course correct. When things aren't going well, the time is right for honest feedback and a two-way dialog. Trying to correct the course midstream can sometimes remove many of the downstream benefits of delegation and turn into a big negative for folks. It not only disempowers, but also demotivates.
- Communicate serendipitously. Don't impede progress. Be careful not to slow

down progress by too many status reports or meetings. Preparing for these can slow down the progress of the task significantly.

- **Availability:**
    - Whether on site or off site, always be available to handle problems in the workplace that need your involvement. Even when on vacation or on a work related trip, always make yourself available 24/7 for those issues that cannot be resolved without your input.
    - Be proactive instead of reactive. Always anticipate problems with any activity or task and try to head off any anticipated problems with proactive action before they become significant and more difficult to resolve.

- Do not spend time fixing what is not broken. Don't blow up everything and start over again. Focus on fixing what is broken and leave alone the parts that are not broken and working well.

- **Affability:**
    - Be persuasive, not intimidating.
    - Be nice. The old saying "you get more with sugar than vinegar" is definitely applicable to the workplace.
    - Be friendly.
    - Be humble.
    - Friendly customer service and customer satisfaction are paramount (applicable to both internal and external customers).

Three B's (Boldness, Beneficial and Belief)

- **Boldness**
    - Think outside the box.
    - Do not think you have to do things the same way because they have always been done that way.
    - Communicate "bad news" immediately. It never gets better with age nor does it ever go away.
    - Reasonable deadlines should be kept.
    - "Carpe Diem" - Seize the opportunity today. Today is the beginning of the future. Tomorrow may be too late.
- **Beneficial**
    - Always think win-win.
    - Anticipate the end result or outcome of an action and how it not only affects you but also others.

- o Ensure every action is positive towards the accomplish of your goals as well as the goals of your organization.
- o Carefully analyze the method of executing an action to insure it does not negatively impact on a colleague, a superior or a subordinate.

- **Belief**
  - o Believe in what you do and how you do it. That is not to say that you are not open to new ways to do things, but insure you believe unequivocally in that new way before you change.
  - o Do not get people in your organization to describe their beliefs publically if you do not agree and want to convince them to change that belief. This only causes embarrassment and humiliation if and when that belief is changed.
  - o On the contrary, if you want people to keep their belief, especially if that belief coincides with

yours, influence them to describe publically. This not only reaffirms their belief but also reinforces yours.

Three C's (Communication, Coordination and Cooperation)

- **Communication**
    - Communication should be constant.
    - It is more than just exchanging information. It's about understanding the emotion and intentions behind the information.
    - It is better to over communicate than not to communicate enough.
    - Never take for granted that a communication is always understood. If there is any doubt, always ask for feedback to insure your message was received and understood.
    - Communication is the glue that helps deepen your connections to others and improves teamwork, decision making and problem solving.
    - Following are barriers to effective communication:

- Stress – When you are stressed or emotionally disturbed, you are more likely to misread people. Take a moment to calm down before continuing your attempt to communicate.

- Lack of focus – When communicating, verbally cease any multitasking. You could miss any non-verbal clues that are prevalent during the conversation. Stop everything else you are doing and stay focused on the communication.

- Inconsistent body language – If you say one thing and your body language say something else; your listener will likely feel that you are being dishonest.

- Negative body language – If you disagree or dislike with what is being said, do not use negative body language, such as

crossing your arms or avoiding eye contact, to express your disagreement. It is better to come out directly and express your disagreement verbally.
- Improving Communication
  - Effective communication is less about talking and more about listening. Do not think about what you are going to say next while the other person is trying to communicate. Listening well means not only understanding the words being said, but also understanding the emotions behind the words.
  - Not only will you better understand the other person by being an engaged listener, but you will also make that person feel more connected and that he or she is being understood.

- By listening attentively, you can also lower the stress level and produce a calming affect if the other person is agitated.
- Avoid interrupting or trying to redirect the conversation to your concerns.
- Show interest in what the other person is saying, even if you do not agree.
- Provide feedback. Say something that will solidify the other person's perception that you understood what he or she was saying. If you do not understand, ask the person to rephrase or further explain.
- Always control your emotions when communicating. Learn how to manage your stress. When you are stressed or emotional you are more likely to misread or misunderstand other people. Plus when

you are stressed or emotional you are more likely to say or do something you will regret later. If you find yourself unable to control your emotion or stress it is better to attempt to excuse yourself, if possible, and renew the conversation another time.
- Be assertive when communicating. Being assertive means expressing your thoughts, feelings and needs in an open and honest way, while standing up for yourself and respecting others.
- Effective communication is always about understanding the other person, not about winning an argument or forcing your opinions on others.

- **Coordination**
    - Teamwork – There is no "I" in the word team.

- Be supportive and compassionate to the feelings of others.
- It is better to over-coordinate than to under-coordinate.
- Following are key elements to coordination:
    - Have a global vision of all the work that has to be done. This is important when dealing with unforeseen changes and aspects that can appear in the future.
    - Set and communicate common goals – you cannot coordinate effectively if all are not on the same page in seeking a common goal.
    - Know the people you are coordinating with. If at all possible, learn their attitude, their motivations and their knowledge.

- Define each person's role when coordinating and insure their role coincides with their expertise.
- Insure effective communication when coordinating.

- **Cooperation**
    - Cooperation increases productivity in the workplace. When everyone is working together towards a common goal, things get done more quickly and efficiently. Cooperation saves time because workers and managers don't have to devote time to bickering and resolving disputes.
    - Cooperation improves job satisfaction. By increasing cooperation among people, workplaces become more welcoming and inviting, thus

improving attitudes and motivations to be more successful in their work.

- In a cooperative workplace, people feel less like drones and more like valuable components in a well-oiled machine. In a cooperative workplace, people are more likely to offer suggestions on how to better accomplish the work. By being allowed to provide productive input, people feel they have a voice in the organization and a stake in its success.
- When workplace cooperation is actively promoted, barriers between people are avoided thus fostering understanding and communication.
- In a cooperative environment always practice the Golden rule – treat people the way you want to be treated.

Conclusion

As you can see, I've outlined these basic principles that I practiced throughout my military and civilian careers in a simple ABC format. These practices have proven successful for me not only in the workplace but also in life in general. Obviously, they are adaptable and can be modified to future environments as the world and its philosophies are ever-changing and evolving, hopefully for the betterment of mankind. You, as the reader, can always adapt and "fine tune" them to fit your particular situation.

Outline Summary (tear out section)

- A's (Ability, Availability and Affability):
    - Ability
        - Attitude + Motivation + Knowledge = Ability to Succeed
            - Attitude
            - Motivation
            - Knowledge
        - Capitalize on the talents of others
        - Earn respect and confidence of others
        - Maintain high motivation and a positive attitude
        - Know what all employees do in an organization
        - Sustain honesty and integrity
        - Loyalty and dedication
        - Fairness to all

- Lead by example
- Capitalize on lessons earned
- KISS – Keep it super simple
- Micro-management should be avoided

- Availability
    - Anticipate and handle problems
    - Be proactive
    - Fix only what's broken

- Affability
    - Do not intimidate
    - Be nice
    - Be friendly
    - Be humble

- B's (Boldness, Beneficial and Belief):
  - Boldness
    - Think outside the box

- Do not resist change if change makes sense
- Communicate bad news immediately
- Seize the opportunity (Carpe diem)
  - Beneficial
    - Think win-win
    - Anticipate outcomes of your action and how it affects others
  - Belief
    - Stick to your beliefs unless it makes sense to change
- C's (Communication, Coordination and Cooperation):
  - Communication
    - Better to over-communicate
    - Insure communication is understood
    - Eliminate barriers

- Always strive to improve communication skills

- Coordination
  - Teamwork
- Cooperation
  - Improves productivity
  - Improves job satisfaction
  - Stimulates new ideas
  - Removes barriers between people
  - Practice the Golden rule

www.ingramcontent.com/pod-product-compliance
Lightning Source LLC
Chambersburg PA
CBHW070402190526
45169CB00003B/1068